Ballerina Betsy

&

Ballerina Bristina

Educational Coloring & Activity Book
Victoria A. Lowell Dansby, Ph. D.

First published in the United States in 2009 by Createspace/Amazon/Impel Books, Inc.

Fourth Edition printed in the United States in 2015 by Createspace/Amazon/Impel Books, Inc.

Copyright © 2009

ISBN: 978-0-615-29314-1

Printed: Createspace/Amazon/Impel Books, Inc.

Library of Congress Cataloging-in-Publication Data

Impel Books, Inc.
Victoria A. Lowell Dansby

Ballerina Betsy & Ballerina Bristina

4

6

I dedicate this project

to

My Mother

and

all the students with whom

I have shared the dancing space!

8

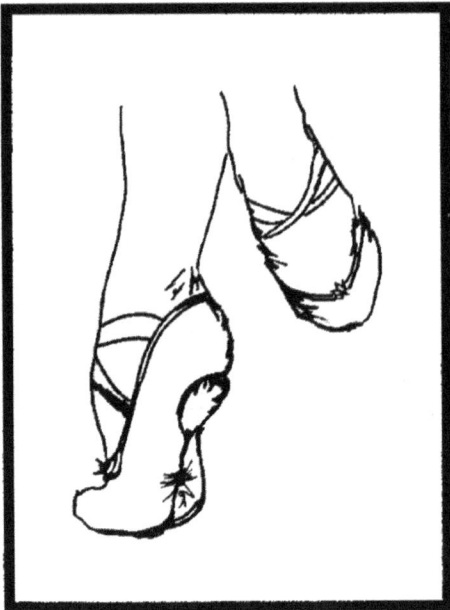

Ballerina Betsy

Ballerina Bristina

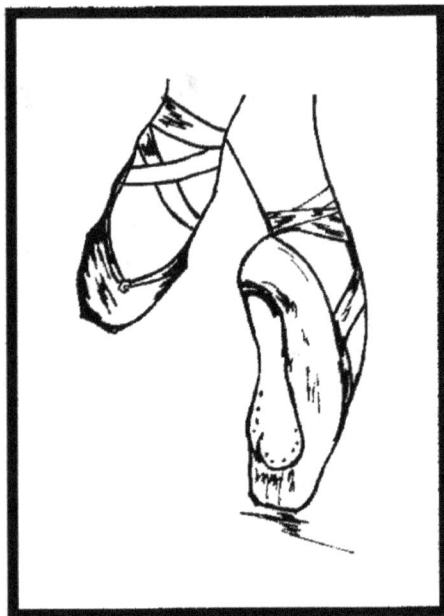

Ballerina Betsy

As Ballerina Betsy performs a demi-plié,

her knees should be positioned:

A.

In front of her feet with her foot rolling
forward

B.

Centered over her toes with all five toes
pressing firmly into the floor

C.

Behind her feet with her foot rolling
backward

Please identify the correct answer by coloring the heart

PINK

Demi – Plié   IstPosition

Do you know your body directions?

Can you identify the body position Betsy is practicing?

Please identify the correct answer by coloring the heart

YELLOW

A.   En Ouvert (open)

B.   En Croisé Derrière (crossed and/or closed)

C.   En Face (facing the audience)

D.   En Ecarté

Battement Tendu Croisé Derrière

Ballerina Betsy

pauses for a moment

in

Sur le cou-de-pied

as she prepares

for her next movement.

Sur le cou-de-pied

Did you know that "Grand Battement," means

"LARGE?"

This movement represents a "large,"

brisk, swinging action of the working leg.

The leg is raised to full extension upward and outward

then returned to the floor closing in 1st or 5th position.

A Grand Battement may be viewed as the continuation of a degagé

in that, you allow the energy of the degage to be released

and the leg to rise to full extension.

Grand Battement à la Seconde

18

Ballerina Betsy extends her arms gracefully,

flowing continuously from one position to another.

This movement phrase has been performed in preparation

for her adagio combination.

Which of the following explanations best defines the term "Adagio?"

Please identify the correct answer by coloring the heart

BLUE

A.   Techniques or actions performed at a swift, staccato tempo, in which the dancer must coordinate the use of the arms, legs, and head to create force and dynamics within the movement phrases.

B.   Movement phrases performed at a slow controlled tempo, in which the dancer must coordinate the use of the arms, legs, and head so that all actions flow from one pose or position to another.

Which style of dancing shoes would

Ballerina Betsy

wear during her ballet class?

Find the correct pair

and

color the heart

PURPLE

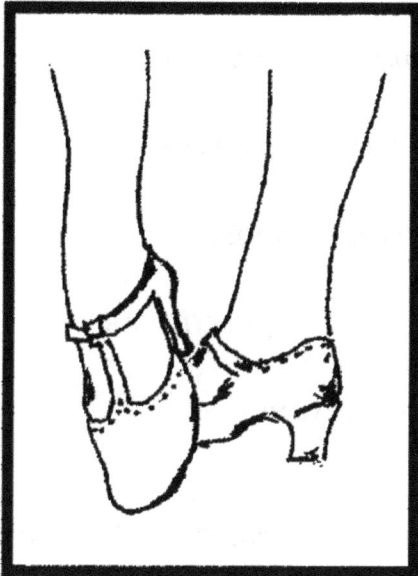

Character Shoes

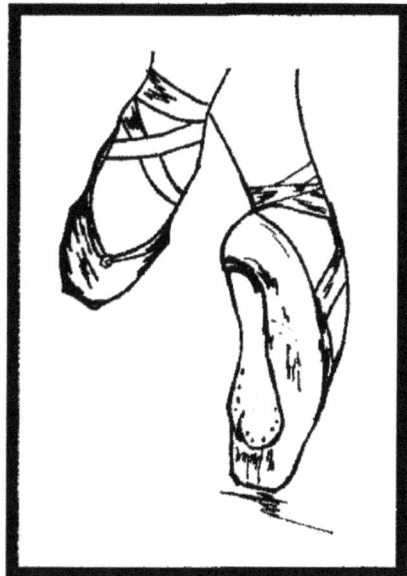

Pointe Shoes

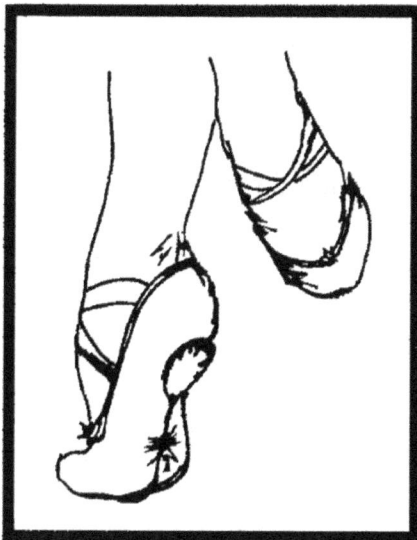

Ballet Slippers

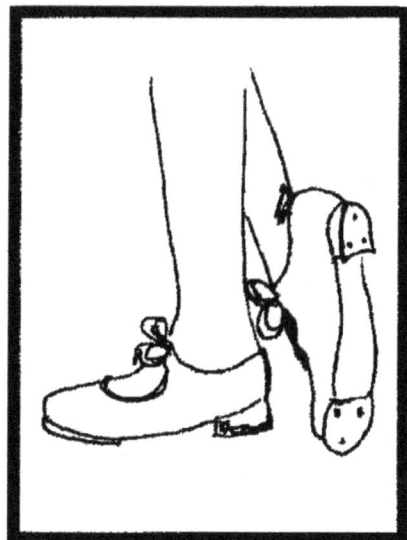

Tap Shoes

Today is ballet class for Ballerina Betsy and her best friend.

They have agreed to meet in the park

and walk to the studio together.

While Betsy waits, she decides to practice her

Battement tendu devant.

Please identify the best explanation by coloring the heart

GREEN

A.   Betsy should brush her foot forward with the heel open and lifted to the front, with the toe turned outward.

B.   Betsy should lead with her toe, brushing forward in a parallel position.

C.   Betsy should turn her foot inward, pointing the heel outward as she brushes forward.

Battement Tendu Devant

Ballerina Betsy enjoys practicing her pirouettes along the

curved, cobblestone pathway of a lush, green meadow.

The following page presents

Betsy executing a left, outside pirouette.

Can you identify the terms for outward and inward rotation,

for the (body, leg, and/or arms)?

Betsy's pirouette is rotating in which direction?

Outside: _____   Inside: _____

Please identify the correct answer by coloring the heart

BLUE

A.   En Dedans

        ♡

B.   En Dehors

        ♡

Pirouette

Which items should Ballerina Betsy

take with her to ballet class?

Find the correct pair

and

color the heart

RED

Leg Warmers

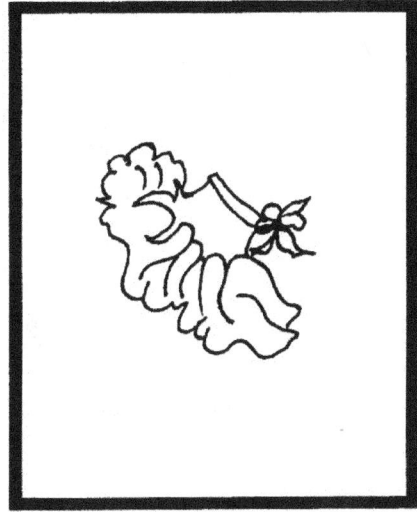

Tutu

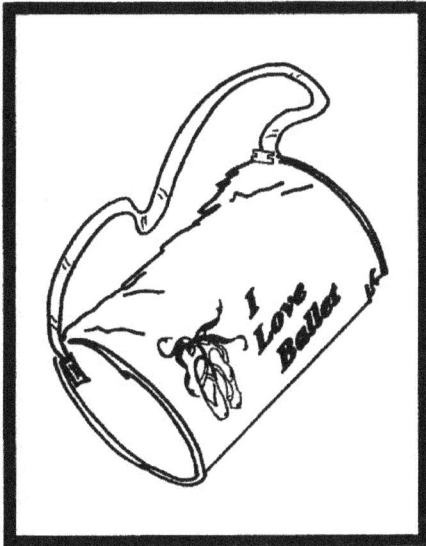

Dance Bag

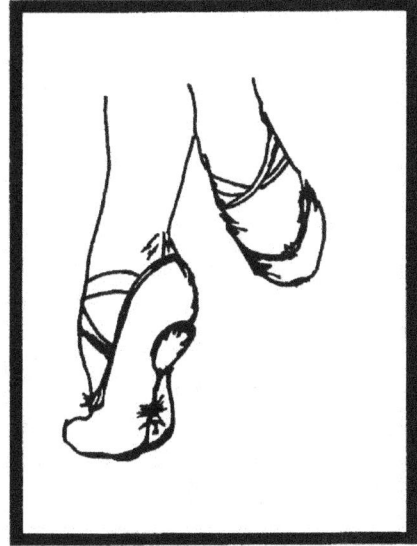

Ballet Slipper

Ballerina Betsy practices her 1ˢᵗ Arabesque.

Did you know that Arabesque

is one of the most well known poses in Classical Ballet?

To perform this elegant position,

a dancer extends one leg behind the body as they maintain

balance on the supporting leg.

Can you identify which arabesque Betsy is performing?

Please identify the correct answer by coloring the heart

PINK

A.   Cecchetti - First Arabesque

♡

B.   French - First Arabesque

♡

C.   Russian (Vaganova) - First Arabesque

♡

1st Arabesque

Arabesque positions will be presented from

the following schools of classical training:

The Cecchetti method of training identifies

a series of five arabesque positions.

The French school identifies two positions and

the Russian (Vaganova) school identifies a series of four

arabesque positions.

Betsy will demonstrate each pose beginning

with 2nd Arabesque - Cecchetti.

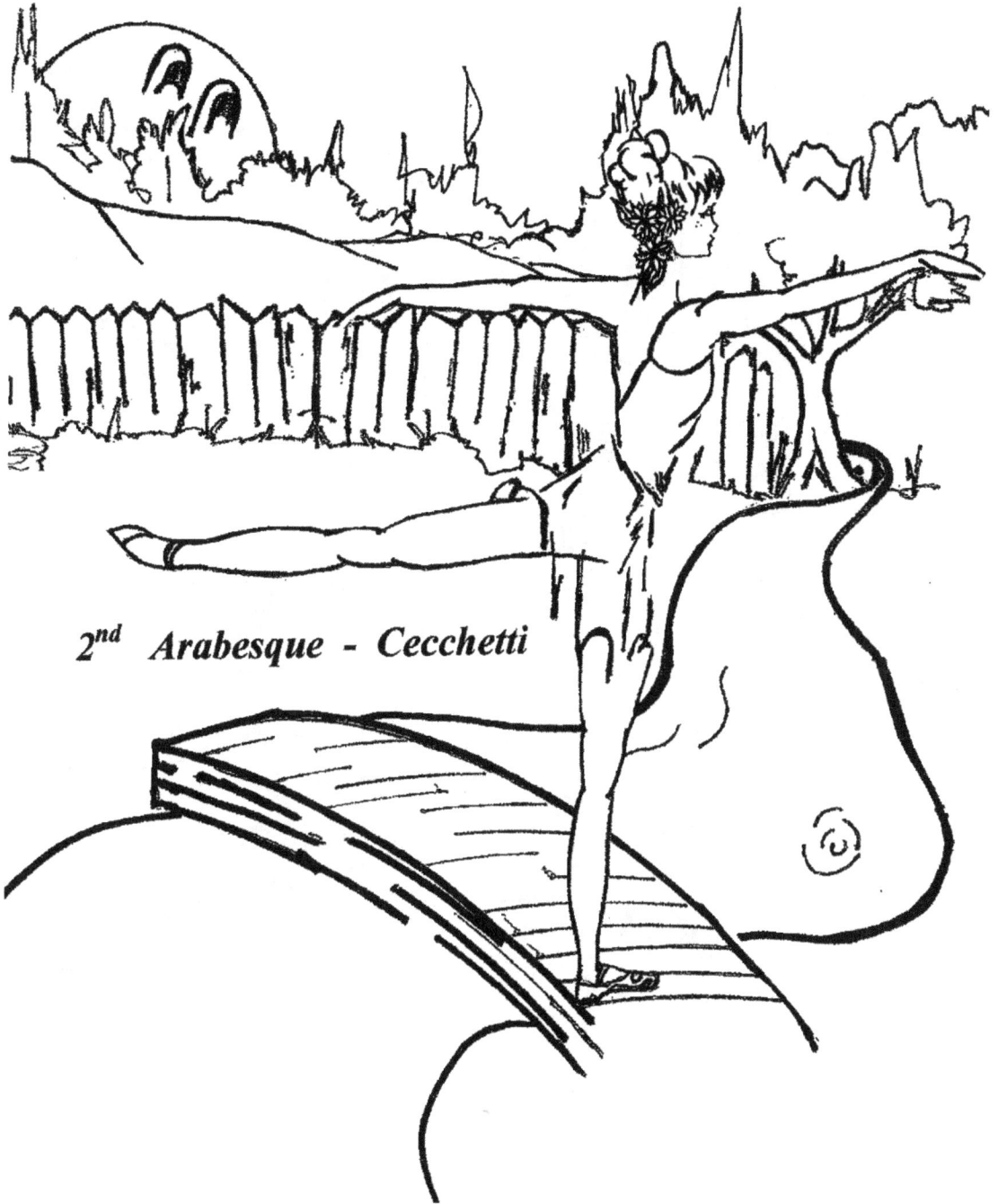

2nd *Arabesque - Cecchetti*

3rd Arabesque - Cecchetti

4th Arabesque - Cecchetti

5ᵗʰ Arabesque - Cecchetti

Arabesque Ouverte - French

Arabesque Croisé - French

1ˢᵗ Arabesque - Russian

2nd Arabesque - Russian

3rd Arabesque - Russian

4th Arabesque - Russian

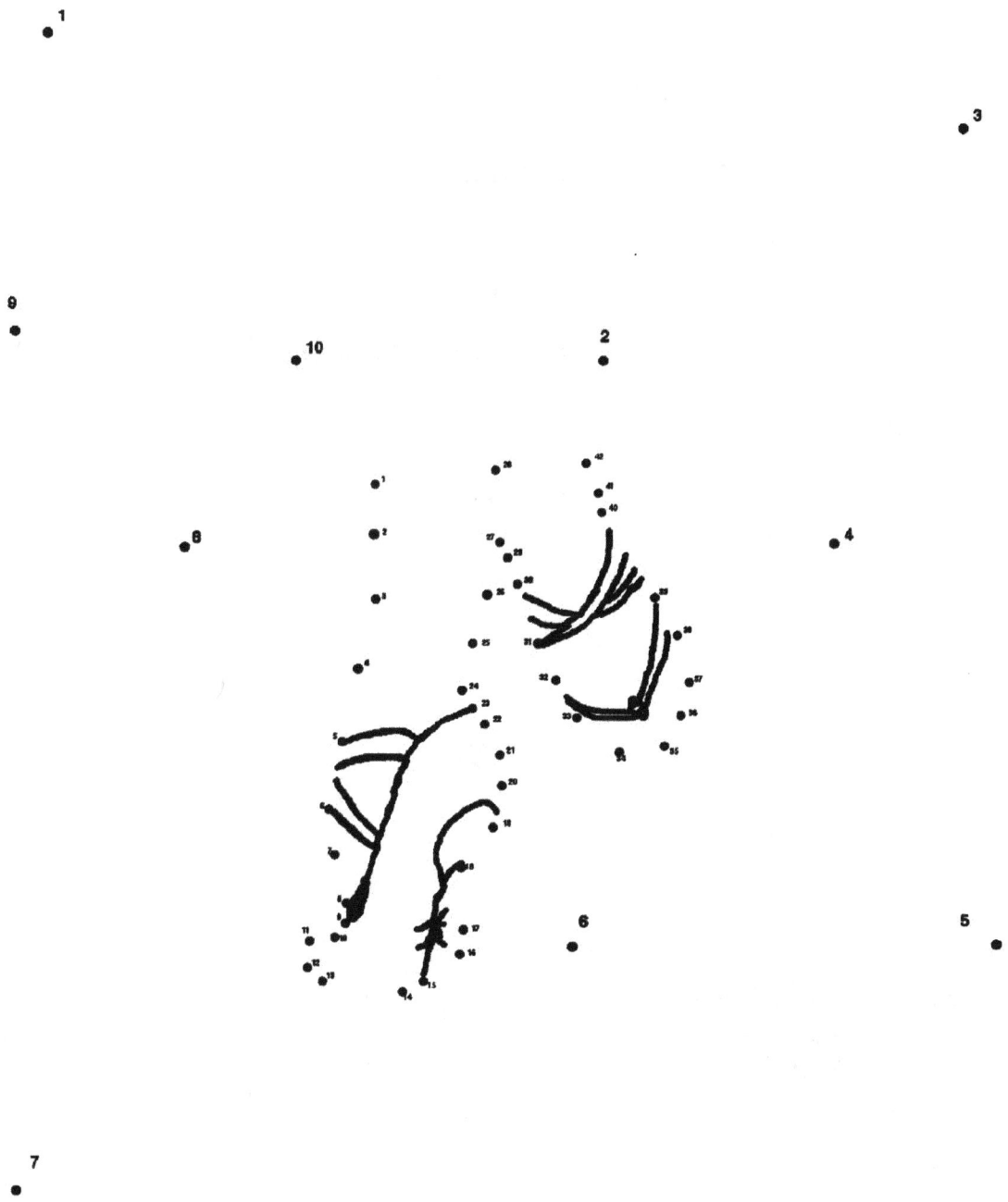

Betsy Feet

Hey diddle diddle,

forget the cat and the fiddle

and

watch Betsy soar over the Moon!

Ballerina Betsy soars through the air as she performs a "Grand Jeté."

Can you identify which of the following movements would assist Betsy

as she initiates the lift of the body into the air?

Please identify the correct answer by coloring the heart

YELLOW

A. *Soutenu*

♡

B. *Grand Battement*

♡

C. *Plié*

♡

Grand Jeté!

Ballerina Betsy springs into the air as she performs

pas de chats.

Do you know what this step represents?

It is the "Step of the Cat."

It was given this name because of its light, cat-like quality.

The pas de chats is a very popular step in many ballets,

for example;

if you watch closely you may see it in Sleeping Beauty,

and in

Swan Lake where the cygnets perform a series of sixteen pas de chats.

Pas de Chats

Mr. Squirt is Ballerina Betsy's best buddy!

He enjoys going to ballet class with her

although, sometimes

he does get in the way!

Ballerina
Bristina

Ballerina Bristina rises to full pointe

as she balances effortlessly in Soussus.

Can you identify the correct definition for the Cecchetti method of execution

and the French technique ?

Please match the correct definition with its school by coloring the hearts

with the identified color then connect with a line.

French   **RED**   **Cecchetti**   **GREEN**

A.   The dancer rises to full pointe with a little spring, distinctly pushing off the floor. This technique develops a more elastic foot and teaches the concentration of balance on one spot.

♡   ♡

French

B.   This technique requires the dancer to move fluidly and smoothly as she rises to full pointe, which strengthens the tendons of the heels and develops control. Most often used with beginning dancers.

♡   ♡

Cecchetti

SOUSSUS

Which pair of dancing shoes should

Ballerina Bristina wear

for her technique class?

Find the correct pair

and

Color the heart PINK

Character Shoes

♡

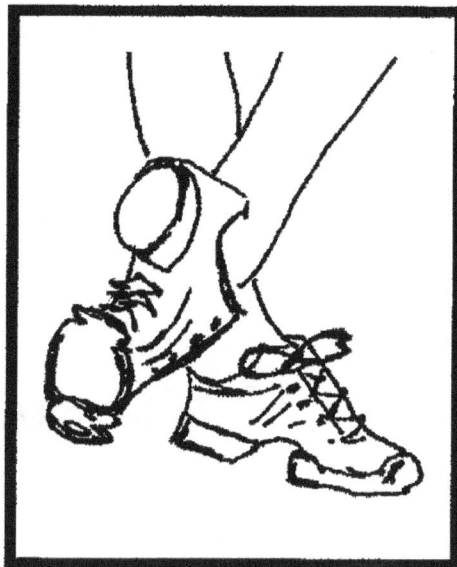

Jazz Sneakers

♡

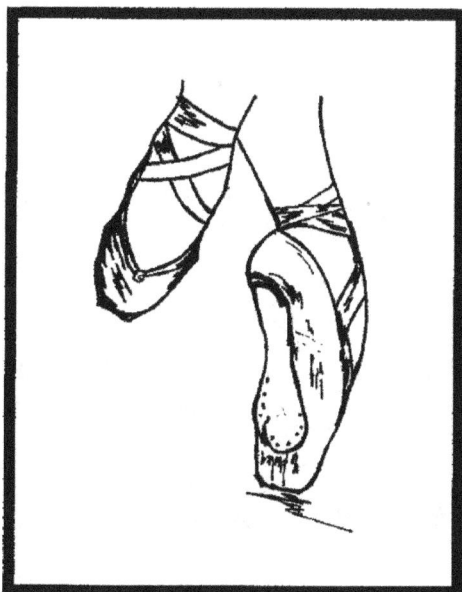

Pointe Shoes

♡

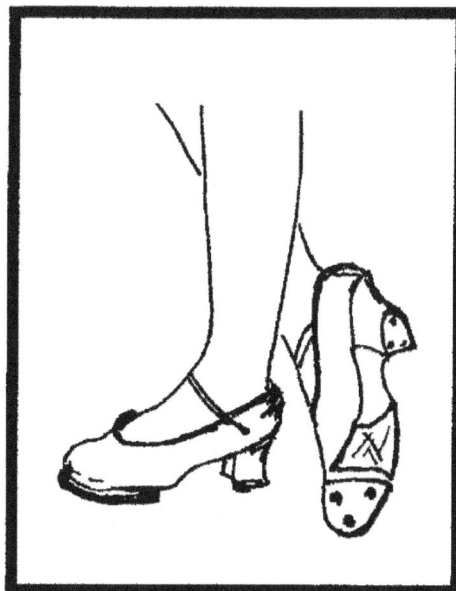

Tap Shoes

♡

Ballerina Bristina springs to a wide 2nd position.

She poses with perfect balance, in relevé à la seconde.

Do you know what the term relevé means?

Relevé means to "lift," or "to rise up."

To perform a relevé à la seconde,

as Bristina has in the example,

a dancer must push off their feet brushing outward

into 2nd position, rising quickly onto demi or full pointe.

Relevé à la Seconde

Ballerina Bristina brushes her downstage leg forward,

executing a battement tendu en croisé devant.

Do you know what the term "croisé" means?

Which of the following explanations best defines the term?

Please identify the correct answer by coloring the heart

PURPLE

A. Position of the body in which the "upstage" leg is the supporting leg. The working leg extends back, and the toe is pointed on floor. Torso and hips are at an oblique angle to the audience, center of the body is open, with torso inclined slightly forward. (open position)

♡

B. Position of the body in which the "upstage" leg is the supporting leg. The working leg extends forward, and the toe is pointed on floor. Torso, and hips at an oblique angle to the audience, center of body is closed off, with torso inclined slightly back. (crossed or closed off)

♡

Battement

Tendu

en Croisé

Ballerina Bristina dances along the banks of the Seine River.

She pauses for a moment near the Eiffel tower,

*posing effortlessly on full pointe. Bristina has executed a "**Piqué**."*

Can you explain the word "Piqué?"

Piqué means (to prick) or

to step directly onto demi or full point?

Do you know where the Eiffel Tower is located?

Please identify the correct answer by coloring the heart YELLOW

A.   Florence, Italy

♡

B.   Leningrad, Russia

♡

C.   Paris, France

♡

The Ballet Comique de la Reine, has often been referred to as the "first ballet,"

however there are differences of opinion as to the definition of "first."

With that said, this legendary event took place at Fontainebleau in 1581

at the court of Henry II of France. This unique production fostered the emergence

of ballet's technical roots, a codified language, and the development of a heritage

that has blossomed into the exquisite art form we admire today.

Piqué

58

Attitude croisé

may be performed in three styles or schools of training.

Do you know which style Ballerina Bristina is performing?

Please identify the correct answer by coloring the heart

PINK

A.   *Cecchetti*

♡   The body and the back are held straight, with the knee held level or slightly lower than the foot.

B.   *French*

♡   The body is slightly forward and titled toward the supporting leg. The knee is held on the same level as the foot . The raised arm includes a lifinting of the same shoulder.

C.   *Russian*

♡   The shoulders are held even, the body is bent back with a slight arch, and the knee is held slightly higher that the foot.

Attitude Croisé

Ballerina Bristina will present six attitude variations:

1.   Attitude Croisé Devant

2.   Attitude Épaulé

3.   Attitude Croisé Derrière - Cecchetti and Russian

4.   Attitude Effacé - Cecchetti and Russian

The attitude position was developed/credited to Carlo Blasis.

Historical record states that

his inspiration for this beautiful position came from

the statue of Mercury.

Attitude Croisé Devant

62

Attitude Épaulé

Attitude Croisé Derrière - Cecchetti

64

Attitude Croisé Derrière - Russian

Attitude Effacé - Cecchetti

Attitude Effacé - Russian

Ballerina

Bristina

Mr. Squirt sits attentively,

*watching Ballerina Bristina perform a **Grand Jeté.***

She appears weightless as she

soars high into the air.

*Did you know **Grand** means big or large?*

Grand Jeté

*Ballerina Bristina completes her Révérence in a deep lunge facing **upstage**.*

Can you identify your stage directions?

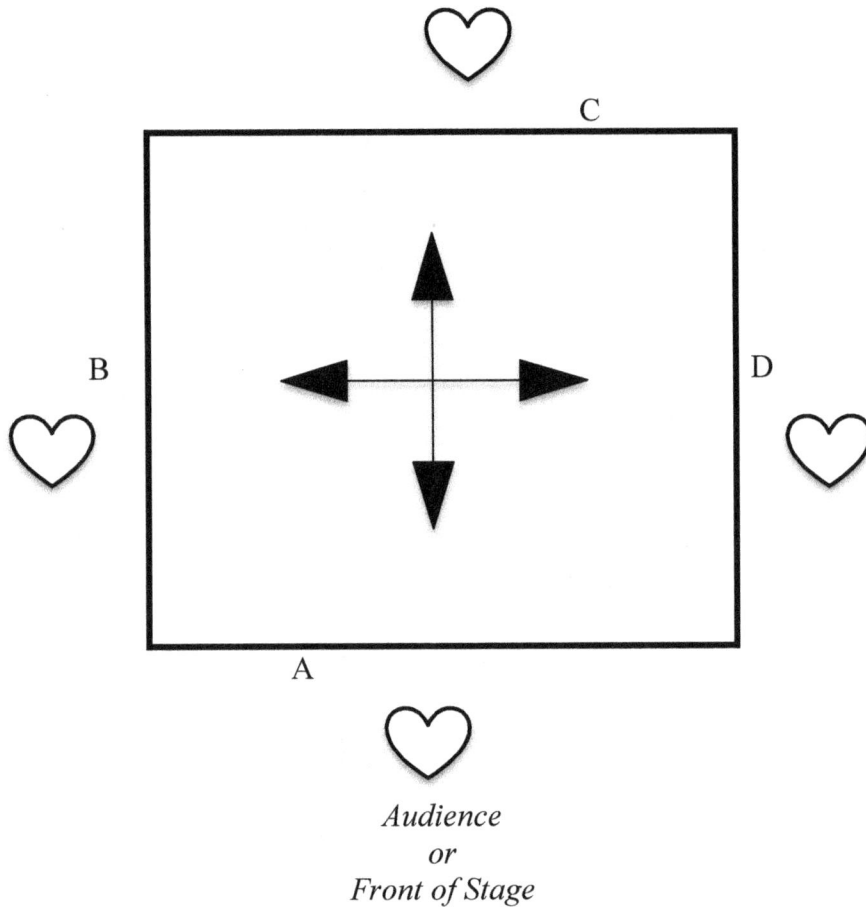

Audience
or
Front of Stage

Please identify the correct answers by coloring the hearts

A.	Downstage	BLUE
B.	Stage-Right	RED
C.	Upstage	GREEN
D.	Stage-left	YELLOW

Ballerina Bristina poses to begin Révérence.

A révérence is the final movement of a dancer's technique class and is performed

by students and the instructor in appreciation of the participants mutual efforts.

This polite tradition is executed as a bow or curtsy and can range in style from

simplistic movement phrases to elaborate choreographic motifs.

Révérence may vary for men and women. For example,

women often step or rond de jambe to the side, gracefully opening the arms

into 2nd position as the other foot is carefully placed behind the supporting foot.

Simultaneously, the legs close, the knees bend,

and the body leans slightly forward from the hips.

A man may simply step forward,

bringing the other foot closed as the knees "soften."

The arms remain at his side, as he bows his head forward.

Ballerina Bristina

is on her way to a very important audition.

She grabs her dance bag

and

darts from the rehearsal studio.

The

End

Answer Key

Page	Answer	
10	B	
12	B	
18	C	
21	Ballet Slippers	
22	A	
24	B	
27	All Items	*Leg warmers, Tutu, Ballet slippers, Dance bag*
28	A	
42	B & C	
48	A to Cecchetti	B to French
51	Pointe Shoes	
54	B	
56	C	
58	B	

Adagio	Refers to slow controlled movements performed to select music that is "slow" and/or sustained in tempo. May be performed by couples or individual dancers. Usually placed during the center section of the lesson and often involves high extensions, holds, and movements that demonstrate flexibility and balance.
Allegro	Refers to light, energetic, springy movements such as leaps, jumps, or skips and is usually performed to music, with a brisk and/or staccato tempo.
Arabesque	"Ornament." Research has shown that the term has been derived from descriptions of intricate Moorish designs. Classified as a "big pose," often demonstrating a dancer's ability to perform in extension movements.
Attitude	"Pose." This position was developed by Carlo Blasis and inspired by the statue of Mercury by Giovanni da Bologna. A dancer achieves this line by raising one leg behind the body to 90 degrees as they bend the knee to form a 75 to 90 degree angle behind the body.
Balancé	A rocking motion in 3/4-waltz time. Step one: The dancer steps to the side into demi-plié, the other leg on the cou-de-pied derrière. Step two: The dancer steps onto demi-pointe on the back leg, as the other leg moves to cou-de-pied devant (front). Step three: The dancer returns to demi-plié on the front leg. The movement is repeated on the other side (up-and-down). Only "one" foot at a time has contact with the floor.
Battement	"Beating." Refers to a number of movements that include a beating action of the leg (frappé, jeté, tendu, petit battement, grand battement, etc.).

Battement tendu	"Stretched or extension." The working leg extends outward until the toes are fully stretched and then returns to the closed positions. During the execution of the "tendu" a dancer's toes <u>always</u> remain in contact with the floor.
Chassé	The "Chasing" step. One foot chases the other: It can be performed moving forward, to the side, and/or backward.
Chat, pas de	"Step of the cat." Beginning in 5th position, the back leg is raised to the Retire position, the other leg pushes off and also rises into the retiré position. At that moment, both feet are off the floor. The landing occurs on the first leg, the second leg closes in front as soon as the landing has occurred.
Coupé	"To cut." A movement used to free the supporting leg, or exchange weight and/or supporting legs. A quick shifting of the weight as the working leg cuts under the supporting leg and replaces legs. A quick shifting of the weight as the working leg cuts under the supporting leg and replaces it (resembles a slight tripping action).
Croisé	"Crossed over." A position, which may be executed in a front or back positional direction of the leg. Action demonstrates the extension of the leg as it is crossed over the central line of the body exhibiting a "closed" position to the audience.
Degagé	"To disengage." The working leg extends outward in a "sharp brushing motion" until the toes are fully stretched and leave the floor (disengaging the contact with the floor), then return to the closed position. During the execution of the degagé, a dancer's toes <u>must rise from the floor approximately 2 inches.</u>

Derrière	A position of the leg to the back either par terre (on the floor) or en l'air (in the air).
Ecarté	"Stretched out wide, separated, thrown wide apart." A position qualifying direction of the leg to the side. The leg nearest the audience is pointed in 2nd position a'terre or en l'air.
Effacé	"Erased or shaded." A position identifying the front or back directions of the leg. This movement is away, opened out from the central line of the body.
En Dedans	Rotation of the body directed inward. As the dancer executes a turn the movements will be toward the leg on which they stand: i.e. if the dancer executed the turn from the right leg, the turn would rotate to the right and/or be a "right" turn.
En Dehors	Rotation of the body "Away" from the supporting leg. A dancer turns "away" from the leg on which they stand.
En face	"Facing straight forward." Body is toward the audience or front of the body is facing downstage.
Grand Jeté	The front leg does a grand battement front at the same time as the back leg pushes off the floor propelling the body upward. In the air, the legs are in a split position, one leg in front, one in the back. Jump over that fence or the mud puddle!
Jeté	"Thrown." A jump, that begins on one leg and lands on the other.
Passé	"Passing." Most often associated with retire: Action that requires the working leg be lifted to the height of the supporting knee and passes from front to close in the back, or vice versa.

Piqué	"Pricked," as with a sharp needle. Piqué is used to describe a lifting and bouncing off the floor with a fully extended leg as the dancer steps onto full pointe.
Pirouettes	"A turn." A spin on demi- or full pointe of one leg while the other is raised to a specific position, in retiré or one of the big poses.
Plié	"Bending" of the knees. Performed in 1st, 2nd, 3rd, 4th, and 5th positions. Demi-plié: Halfway to a full bending of the knees, heels remain on the floor in all positions. Grand plié: Full bending of the knees. In 2nd position the heels remain on the floor; in the other positions the heels are allowed to rise slightly after the depth of the demi-plié has been reached.
Pointe	"On the toes." The weight rests on the tips of the toes of fully pointed feet.
Port de bras	"A movement of the arms," from one position to the other.
Promenade	A movement on one leg, the other raised, whereby the body rotates around the central point of the supporting foot. The movement or rotation for the promenade is initiated from the supporting heel. To rotate forward-en dedans, the dancer will lift and shift the heel forward in small increments, which propels the body in a circular motion forward. To initiate the rotation backward or en dehors, the dancer will lift and shift the heel backwards in small increments, which propels the body in a backwards direction.
Relevé	"Lifted." Describes the movement of a straight leg when the heels are lifted off the floor (sometimes referred to as elevé), as in battement relevé. Also refers to the springing motion onto demi- or full pointe, either on one leg or on both, as in passé relevé (on one foot) or soussus (on both feet).

82

Révérence	"To give respect." An obedient bow or curtsy, performed at the completion of the class, exhibiting respect for the instructor and the discipline.
Sauté	"Jumped." Qualifies movements that can be done with a jump.
Seconde	A position of the leg to the side, either par terre (on the floor) or en l'air (in the air).
Soussus	Soussus is a relevé in the fifth position performed sur place or traveled forward, backward or to the side. The dancer springs onto demi or full-point, drawing the feet and legs tightly together. (see relevé)
Sur le cou-de-peid	*"To Wrap"* Devant foot positioning: The working foot is wrapped around the ankle, just above the anklebone. The heel touches the ankle and the toes touch the back of the supporting heel. Derrière foot positioning: The heel touches the back of the supporting ankle, and the toes point away from the supporting leg. The working foot is slightly flexed at the ankle, but the instep is fully pointed (flexed, ankle-pointed toe).

References

Hammond, S. N.   2004. Ballet basics, 5th edition. New York: McGraw-Hill companies, Inc.

Kirstein, L. and Stuart, M.   1952. The classic ballet: Basic technique and terminology. Gainesville: University Press of Florida.

Lawson, J.   Ballet class: Principles and practice. New York: Theatre Arts Books.

Mara, T.   1987. First steps in Ballet: Basic exercises at the barre. Princeton: Book Company.

Page, R.   1984. Class: Notes on dance classes around the world. Princeton Book Company.

Shook, K.   1977. Elements of classical ballet technique. Princeton Book Company.

Vaganova, A.   1969. Basic principles of classical ballet. Translated by Anatole Chujoy. New York: Dover Books.

www.ingramcontent.com/pod-product-compliance
Lightning Source LLC
Chambersburg PA
CBHW080525030426
42337CB00023B/4635